Your Life as a PIONEER on the OREGON TRAIL

by Jessica Gunderson

illustrated by Rachel Dougherty

PICTURE WINDOW BOOKS

a capstone imprint

Thanks to our advisers for their expertise, research, and advice:

Kevin Byrne, PhD, Professor of History
Gustavus Adolphus College, Saint Peter, Minnesota

Terry Flaherty, PhD, Professor of English
Minnesota State University, Mankato

Editor: Jill Kalz
Designer: Ashlee Suker
Art Director: Nathan Gassman
Production Specialist: Danielle Ceminsky
The illustrations in this book were created with acrylics.

Picture Window Books
1710 Roe Crest Drive
North Mankato, MN 56003
877-845-8392
www.capstonepub.com

Library of Congress Cataloging-in-Publication Data
Gunderson, Jessica.
  Your life as a pioneer on the Oregon Trail / by Jessica Gunderson ;
illustrated by Rachel Dougherty.
        p. cm. — (The way it was)
  Includes index.
  ISBN 978-1-4048-7157-1 (library binding)
  ISBN 978-1-4048-7250-9 (paperback)
  1. Pioneer children—Oregon National Historic Trail—Juvenile
literature. 2. Oregon National Historic Trail—Juvenile literature.
3. Pioneers—Oregon National Historic Trail—Social life and
customs—Juvenile literature. 4. Frontier and pioneer life—West
(U.S.)—Juvenile literature. 5. Overland journeys to the
Pacific—Juvenile literature. I. Dougherty, Rachel, 1988– ill.
II. Title.
  F597.G86 2012
  978—dc23   2011029593

Printed in the United States   5547

YOUR ROLE

Congratulations! You'll be playing the role of Abigail Cross in our play "Life on the Oregon Trail." The year is 1847. You, your husband, and your three children are heading west across North America to start a new life. And you're not alone. Hundreds of other families are traveling with you.

The five-month-long journey will be hard. You'll cross unsettled wilderness and steep mountains. You'll battle nightmarish insects. But at the end, you'll find a new home.

Ready?

Westward ho!

OREGON OR BUST

It's a sunny May day in Independence, Missouri. It's crowded, and your children—Frankie, Henry, and Jenny—keep running off. Do you have everything you'll need? Flour, bacon, and beans? Check. Medicine and tools? Check. Your mother's china? Check. Your antique table? Check. Children? Where are the children? A bugle sounds.

"Kids, come back here!" you yell.
"We're leaving!"

In 1847 "Oregon Country" was made up of present-day Oregon, Washington, Idaho, and parts of Montana and Wyoming. Oregon became a state in 1859.

This is no small adventure, my dear! A wagon train could carry 1,000 people. Some wagon trains were nearly 3 miles (4.8 kilometers) long!

ROUGH RIDING

After leaving Missouri, you travel over the plains. At first you ride inside while your husband, Jim, leads the oxen. But the ride is very rough. You think it's probably better to walk.

Outside the wind is fast and heavy, and your skirt fusses and flaps. You wish you could wear pants like the men.

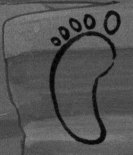

Almost every Oregon Trail pioneer walked—even kids—for most of the 2,000-mile (3,219-km) trip. Some rode horses, but many people didn't have enough money to buy them.

Sorry, Abigail, no pants for you. Women in those days wore long dresses with long sleeves. Oh, and I hope you really like what you're wearing. You have only **one** other dress in the wagon. There's simply no room for more.

COLD LUNCH

At noon the wagons stop for a break. There's no time to cook, so you feed your family dry bread and coffee. The kids whine. **"We'll have better food tonight,"** you promise, though you know it's probably not true.

After just one morning of travel, you're covered in dust. You all are. You lead the kids to the Platte River. The water is so cold, though, that no one wants to bathe. "I guess we just have to be dirty," you tell them.

The wagons' large wheels kicked up a lot of dust. The wagons at the end of the train had the worst of it. Wagons changed places in line every day. This practice made sure no one had to suffer more dust than others.

CAMPING OUT

Some of the men scout ahead for a good camping place. At six o' clock the wagons corral, or make a circle. You soak the beans and start a fire. You hang a kettle over the flame to fry the bacon and cook the beans. Jenny wrinkles her nose. "Better get used to it," you tell her. "It's all we brought."

Sometimes pioneers left wooden markers along the trail. The markers gave other travelers tips, such as the best places to camp or find water.

Most families packed about 200 pounds
(91 kilograms) of flour and 50 pounds (23 kg)
of bacon per person. They also took beans,
rice, coffee, and cooking basics, such as salt
and sugar. Food supplies alone in each wagon
weighed an average of 1,700 pounds (771 kg).

NIGHT ON THE PRAIRIE

Bedtime! The wagon is too small for all of you, so you lie outside. Just as you're drifting off, you feel something slither along your foot.

You scream.
Everyone in the wagon wakes up.
A harmless garter snake scuttles away. "Sorry, false alarm!" you call, embarrassed.

One or several men guarded the camp each night from wild animals such as bears and mountain lions. There was also the fear of an American-Indian attack. But very few such attacks happened.

In a blink it's time to get up. You start the fire for breakfast while Jim leads the oxen to graze. Shortly after sunrise the wagon train readies to leave. "Mama, I have to go," says Jenny. You hurry with her into the trees. You hope you'll be able to catch up to the other wagons.

Don't panic, dear! The wagons travel pretty slowly, averaging 15 miles (24 km) a day. But don't fall too far behind, or you may get lost.

Buffalo Chips Are Not for Eating

Sometimes the prairie is black with herds of buffalo. You and the kids look for buffalo dung—hard, crispy discs you call **"buffalo chips."** The chips burn hotter and longer than wood, which is becoming scarce. You put them in your apron and try not to think about what they really are.

Kids on the trip had to help with many chores, but they had fun too. They played ball games or leap-frog and tag. They picked flowers and went exploring.

Ever eaten buffalo meat, Abigail? It tastes a lot like beef. Sadly, buffalo were nearly extinct by the 1900s. White settlers had overhunted them.

The kids have a different idea. "**How far will it fly?**" Frankie asks, flinging one of his chips into the air. Henry laughs and joins in too. Even Jenny flings hers. It sails into the river with a plop. "**That's not ladylike!**" you cry.

Passing the Time

In the evening you and Jenny wash clothes in the Platte River. The water is cold, and your hands sting from the harsh soap. Back at camp Frankie and Henry build the cooking fire. You have to admit, the buffalo chips give the bacon and beans a nice smoky flavor.

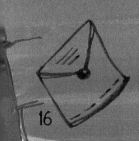

The wagon trains were largely on their own. But there were a few U.S. forts along the trail. Fort Kearny and Fort Laramie were two. Pioneers could mail letters and buy supplies there.

After dinner the kids read by the firelight. It's the only schooling they'll get until Oregon. Your husband brings out his fiddle, and everyone dances.

On the plains, pioneers sometimes dug holes for their fires. If they didn't, the wind would blow out the flames.

PAWNEE TRADE

One day you see riders in the distance. You don't know if they're friendly. Jim grabs his gun, just in case. You order the kids into the wagon.

But the Pawnee Indians are friendly. They want to trade. You admire the beading on the women's blouses. You give the visitors some flour in exchange for a buffalo-hide robe and beads. The Pawnee also have good information. They point the way to elk hunting grounds.

Most American-Indian tribes were peaceful toward the pioneers. But in the late 1850s, as more settlers headed west, some tribes charged fees to pass through. And sometimes there was fighting on both sides.

CRACKING THE WHIP

The next day Jim goes off to hunt. He leaves you in charge of the wagon. Henry wants to learn how to lead, so you let him. "Giddyup," he tells the oxen. But they don't move.

"Crack the whip, son," you tell him. He swings the whip over the oxen's heads, and they plod forward. But the train is curving left, and the oxen want to go straight. "Left!" he shouts. "Left!"

Some pioneers used mules instead of oxen to pull their wagons. Mules could be harnessed rather than led. But they cost more than oxen.

20

Let me give you some advice, Henry. To make the oxen turn left, yell "Haw!" To get them to turn right, yell "Gee!" To stop, yell "Whoa!"

RAIN AND BUGS AND DISEASES, OH MY!

Sometimes you trudge through rain. Sometimes you wake covered with mosquitoes. Giant beetles buzz by your head. "I'm hungry," Frankie says every day. "I'm thirsty," Henry whines. "My skin itches!" Jenny cries. "I'm sorry, children," you say. "But look on the bright side. You don't have cholera!"

The oxen are tired, and you're not even halfway to Oregon. "Time to lighten the load," Jim tells you. You leave your antique table in the weeds. You know it's only a table, but you tear up just the same.

Cholera was the deadliest disease on the trail. It spread quickly from person to person and killed thousands. Accidents were another major cause of death. People were sometimes run over by wagons.

Remember your medicine bag, dear! You've got hartshorn for insect bites and snakebites. You've got laudanum for pain and camphor for the common cold. And remember to boil water before drinking it. Boiling water can kill the bacteria that cause cholera. Sadly, most pioneers didn't know this at the time.

RIVER CROSSING

It's time to cross the North Platte River. You're excited, but nearly everyone else is terrified. You can swim, but most other pioneer women can't (it's not ladylike!). Neither can your kids.

The men herd the animals through the water. Then they build rafts to float the wagons across. You climb in the wagon and hold on for dear life. The wagon tips and almost topples. Your china falls into the water. **"At least we've lightened the load,"** you say, trying to be cheerful.

Some pioneers and American Indians made a business out of river crossings. They built ferries or bridges and charged travelers a fee to cross.

Here's a tip, my dear. Cross the river late in the day, when the animals are tired. Animals are friskier in the morning and might run away rather than obey.

CHINA

MOUNTAINS

You come upon a great rock called Independence Rock. It's the halfway point! You and the kids climb it and carve your names. Several weeks later you reach the mountains.

The phrase "I'm stumped" started on the Oregon Trail. Wagon axles would often break if the wagon hit a large tree stump or rock. A broken axle meant a wagon couldn't move.

The oxen strain to pull the wagons uphill. Going up is hard, but coming back down is worse. You tie ropes to the wagons, and everyone, even the women, helps to lower them slowly down the slope. You hold tightly to the rope. Your feet slip, and sweat drips from your brow. **"This isn't ladylike,"** you mutter.

OREGON

"Are we there yet?," Henry asks in October. And you are! After five long months, you've reached the Willamette Valley in Oregon Country. Your feet won't stop throbbing, and you've lost some of your belongings, but you're alive. "We're home!" you tell him. "At long last."

The pioneers didn't always stay in the Willamette Valley. Some went south to present-day California. Others retraced their steps to settle in present-day Montana or Wyoming.

TAKE A BOW

Wonderful performance! You made it to the end of the Oregon Trail. Long journey, wasn't it? Now you can stop trying to be a lady and go back to being a kid.

Just don't start playing Frisbee with buffalo chips, OK?

In 1869 a cross-country railroad was completed. People moving west began taking trains rather than wagons. Travel on the Oregon Trail became less and less common.

Glossary

axle—a bar in the center of a wheel around which a wheel turns

bacteria—very tiny creatures that live in soil, water, and living things; bacteria can cause disease

camphor—a tough, gummy substance from the camphor tree that is used in medicine

cholera—an illness marked by vomiting, diarrhea, and stomach cramps

extinct—no longer living anywhere on Earth

harness—to fit an animal with gear that allows a person better control of it

hartshorn—a substance made from the horns of a red deer

laudanum—a pain-killing medicine

pioneer—a person who is among the first to settle a new land

Index

More Books to Read

Dunn, Joeming. *The Oregon Trail.* Graphic History. Edina, Minn.: Magic Wagon, 2009.

Friedman, Mel. *The Oregon Trail.* A True Book. New York: Children's Press, 2010.

Wadsworth, Ginger. *Words West: Voices of Young Pioneers.* New York: Clarion Books, 2003.

Internet Sites

FactHound offers a safe, fun way to find Internet sites related to this book. All of the sites on FactHound have been researched by our staff.

Here's all you do:

Visit *www.facthound.com*

Type in this code: 9781404871571

 **Super-cool stuff!** Check out projects, games and lots more at **www.capstonekids.com**

Look for All the Books in the Series: